SECRETS OF ANIMAL CAMOUFLAGE

LOOK AGAIN

STEVE JENKINS AND ROBIN PAGE

Houghton Mifflin Harcourt • Boston • New York

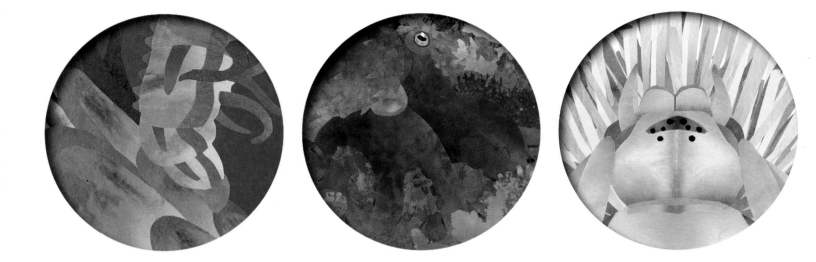

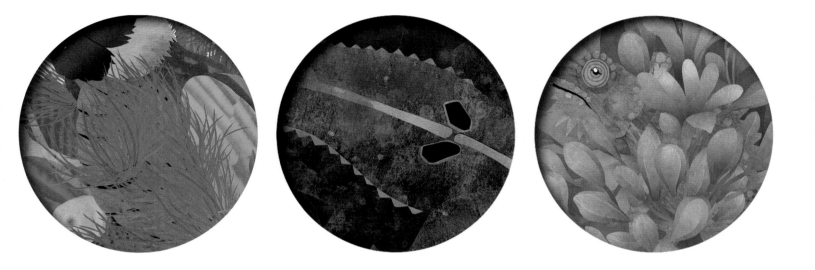

Staying alive can be a challenge for an animal in the wild. Many creatures face the constant threat of being eaten by bigger and stronger animals. And even the fiercest hunters must find prey or they will starve. Staying hidden, whether from predators or prey, is one way to stay alive. And many animals do this surprisingly well.

Colorful coral reefs and dense forests of kelp—a kind of seaweed—are found in shallow ocean waters in many parts of the world. These habitats provide food and shelter to more different kinds of animals than almost any place on earth.

Many coral reef and kelp forest animals are masters of disguise, blending in with the colors and textures of their surroundings. Some do this to avoid being eaten. Others do it to fool their prey.

The **crocodile fish** lurks on the sea floor until a shrimp or small fish comes near. Then it swallows its prey in a single gulp.

The **whip coral shrimp** looks just like a piece of the soft coral it lives on.

The **trumpetfish** hovers upside down to blend in with fronds of coral. When a smaller fish swims by, this sneaky predator lunges and grabs it.

The **leafy seadragon** hides from danger by imitating a piece of floating seaweed.

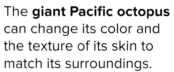

The **frogfish's** colorful camouflage helps it hide from predators—and surprise its prey.

The **giant Pacific octopus** can change its color and the texture of its skin to match its surroundings.

Roots, leaves, and branches—
each part of a tree is a
different habitat. Tree bark, and
the moss and algae that grow
on it, provides a home or resting
place for a variety of animals.

Even living high above the ground can be risky—snakes, birds, and other predators are a constant threat. The best defense? Look like part of the tree.

To most predators, the **moss mimic stick insect** looks like an unappetizing bit of vegetation.

Until it opens its big yellow eyes, the **common potoo's** imitation of a dead tree branch is spot-on.

The **tulip-tree beauty moth** almost disappears on a lichen-covered tree trunk.

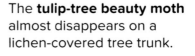

Clinging to the nooks and crannies of a tree's rough bark, the **gray tree frog** stays camouflaged as it searches for ants and other insects to eat.

Flowers produce nectar and pollen—foods that attract insects, birds, and bats. For some creatures, these blossoms are also a colorful place to hide.

Some animals sip flower nectar. Others prey on creatures that are attracted to blossoming plants. And a few fool their enemies by concealing themselves among the petals.

The **high-casqued chameleon** can alter its color to match its environment. This lizard also changes color to send messages to other chameleons.

The **white-banded crab spider** waits, motionless, to seize an unsuspecting bee or butterfly. This spider changes its color to imitate the flower it clings to.

The **orchid mantis** is a fierce predator. As its name suggests, it impersonates a flower, a trick that lures other insects to their doom.

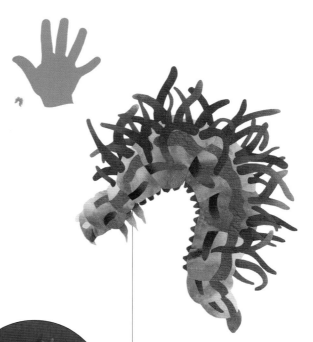

The caterpillar of the **wavy-lined emerald moth** camouflages itself by attaching flower petals to its body.

The bright yellow scales of the **eyelash viper** conceal this snake as it coils among colorful fruit and flowers and waits for its prey.

The colorful feathers of the **rainbow lorikeet** blend in with the flowers of its forest home.

The leaves and plant debris that cover the forest floor offer the animals that live there lots of ways to conceal themselves.

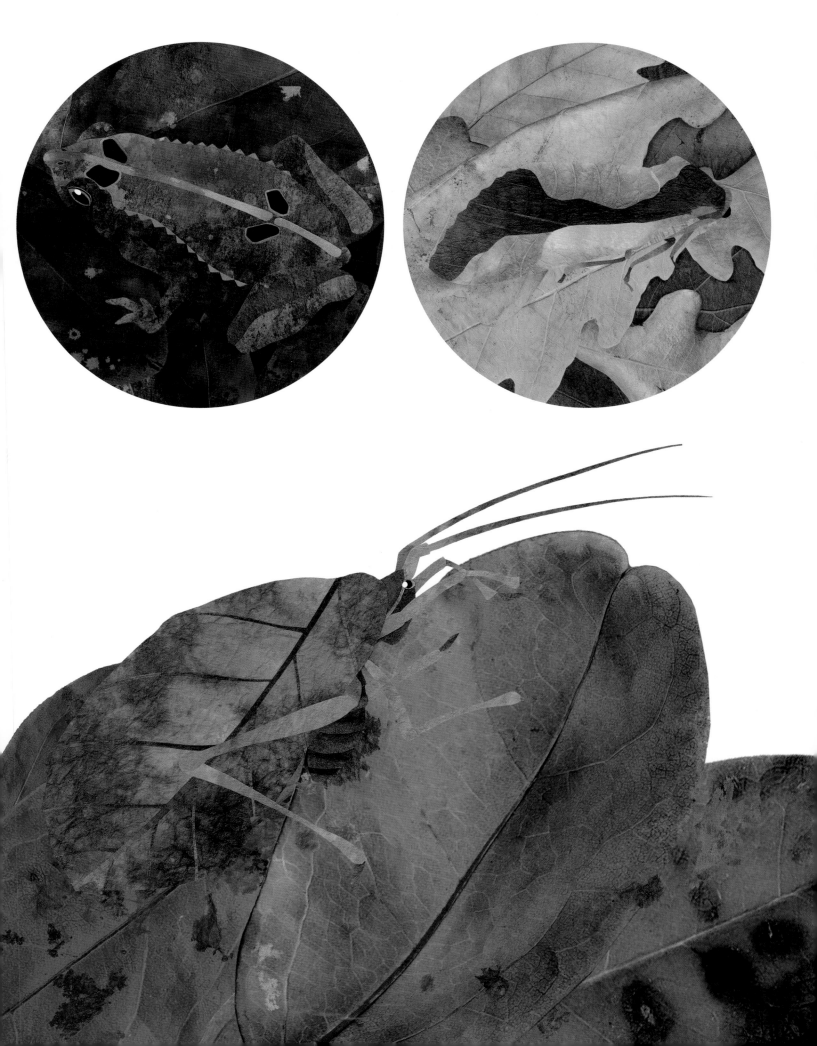

Many of these creatures are a dull color to blend in with the dirt and leaf litter of the forest floor. A few go a step further, imitating dead leaves with impressive accuracy.

The **Gaboon viper** lies quietly among fallen leaves. When a bird or other small animal wanders by, it strikes with its long, venomous fangs.

The coat of a young **Malayan tapir** matches the patterns of light and shadow on the forest floor.

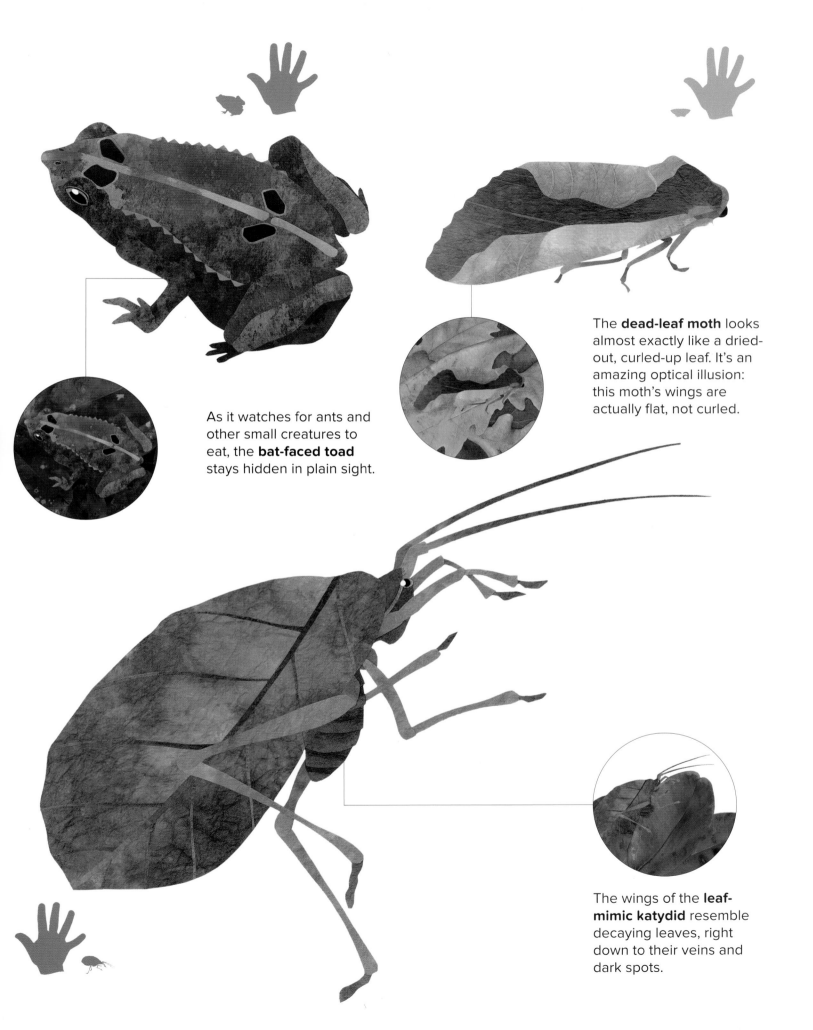

As it watches for ants and other small creatures to eat, the **bat-faced toad** stays hidden in plain sight.

The **dead-leaf moth** looks almost exactly like a dried-out, curled-up leaf. It's an amazing optical illusion: this moth's wings are actually flat, not curled.

The wings of the **leaf-mimic katydid** resemble decaying leaves, right down to their veins and dark spots.

The harsh landscape of the Arctic is covered by snow and ice for much of the year. It's a challenging place for an animal that needs to stay out of sight.

For these creatures, staying hidden means being mostly white—at least when the ground is covered with snow.

The **willow grouse** nests in the trees, where its patterned feathers help it stay hidden.

Like many of the animals that live in snowy habitats, the **Arctic hare** is brown in the summer and white in the winter.

The warm, thick fur of the **Arctic fox** also changes color, turning from brown in the summer to white as snow in the winter.

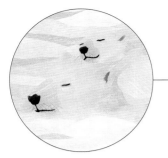

The **polar bear's** white coat allows it to sneak up on the seals it hunts. Some people have reported that the polar bear covers its black nose with a paw when it hunts, but most scientists believe that this is a myth.

Leaves and vines can provide food, shelter, and—for some creatures—a handy hiding place.

Looking like part of a plant can be a good survival strategy for both predators and prey. Some of these creatures have almost perfect disguises.

As it hangs from a tree branch and sways in the breeze, the caterpillar of the **elm sphinx moth** looks like a curled-up dead leaf.

Even the legs of the **giant leaf insect** look like part of a plant. The brown patches on its body, which resemble a decaying leaf, add to the realism.

The **green huntsman spider** lurks in the foliage as it waits for an unwary insect to wander by.

It's not hard to see how the **green vine snake** got its name. This snake lives in the trees, where it hunts birds and other small animals.

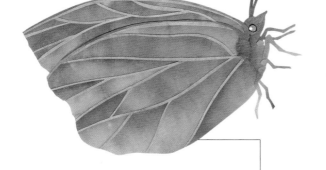

The **common brimstone butterfly** mimics the leaves of the plants it feeds on. If it's disturbed, it holds very still and tucks in its legs, making it look even more like a leaf.

The **marsh frog** isn't easy to spot as it drifts in the water among lily pads and other water plants.

Is that a bunch of dead leaves? No—it's a **satanic leaf gecko**, a master of disguise.

Survival can be a challenge in a rocky environment, where there is little vegetation to hide in.

These creatures have adapted to life in the open by imitating the color and texture of their harsh habitat.

As it rests on the rocky ground of its desert home, the **Namibian stone grasshopper's** disguise makes it almost invisible.

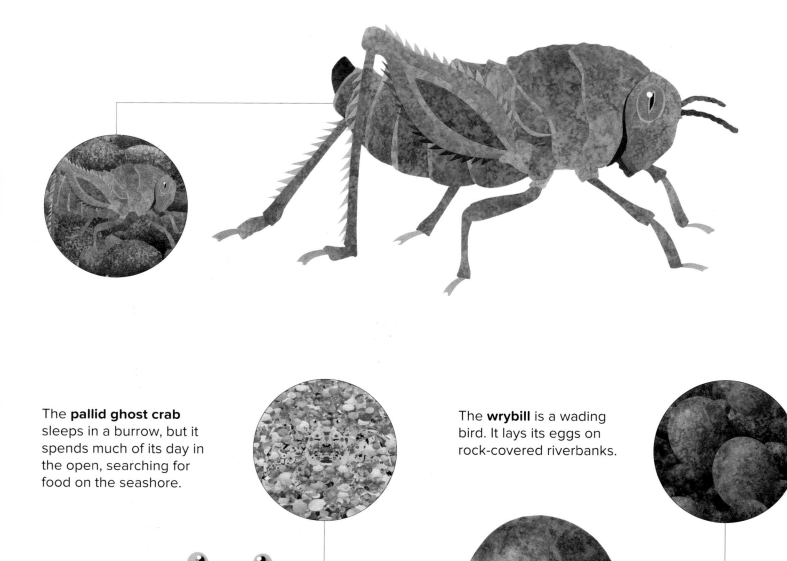

The **pallid ghost crab** sleeps in a burrow, but it spends much of its day in the open, searching for food on the seashore.

The **wrybill** is a wading bird. It lays its eggs on rock-covered riverbanks.

A basking **marine iguana** looks like part of the rock it rests on.

On the following pages, you can learn more about the creatures in this book.

Coral reefs and kelp forests

The **crocodile fish** is found in the southwest Pacific Ocean and the tropical waters of the western Atlantic Ocean. It can reach 20 inches (51 centimeters) in length. This fish makes its home on the sea floor, where it hunts fish, shrimp, and other small sea creatures.

The **whip coral shrimp** clings to the colorful coral that gives it its name. It also shares sea floor burrows with other animals, paying rent by keeping the burrow clean. This small crustacean is about one-half inch (1¼ centimeters) long. It lives on coral reefs in the Indo-Pacific Ocean and feeds on algae and plankton.

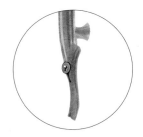

The **trumpetfish** is an ambush hunter. It waits for its prey—smaller fish—as it imitates coral or sea plants.

It also swims behind a larger, harmless fish as a way to sneak up on its victims. Trumpetfish live in the warm waters of the eastern Atlantic Ocean and reach 30 inches (76 centimeters) in length.

Found only in the waters of southern Australia, the **leafy seadragon's** disguise keeps it safe from predators. These fish are about nine inches (23 centimeters) long. They eat plankton and small shrimp. The female leafy seadragon attaches her eggs to the male's tail. He will carry them until they hatch.

When a fish, shrimp, or other small animal gets close, the **frogfish** swallows it whole. Found in tropical waters throughout the world's oceans, this fish grows to 12 inches (30 centimeters) in length. It can change color to match its surroundings.

The **giant Pacific octopus** is one of the world's largest

invertebrates—animals without a backbone. With its arms spread, it can be as much as 16 feet (5 meters) across. These huge mollusks inhabit the waters of the northern Pacific Ocean, where they feed on fish, crabs, clams, and other sea creatures.

Trees

The **moss mimic stick insect** hides from predators by imitating a moss-covered twig. It makes its home in the tropical rainforests of Central and South America, where it feeds on algae and decaying plants. It is a large insect, up to seven inches (18 centimeters) long.

At night, the **common potoo** feeds on beetles and other insects. It sleeps during the day, perched on a dead tree branch. Special eyelids allow it to peek through a slit and watch for danger without revealing its bright yellow eyes. Potoos are found throughout much of Central and South America. They are about 15 inches (38 centimeters) long.

The **tulip-tree beauty moth** lives in the forests of the eastern United States. At night, it feeds on plant pollen and nectar. During the day it rests on tree trunks and branches, where its camouflaged wings and body keep it hidden from predators. This moth has a wingspan of up to two inches (5 centimeters).

The **gray tree frog** lives near ponds and marshes throughout the eastern United States and Canada. These little frogs grow to be about two inches (5 centimeters) long. They spend most of their lives in the treetops, where they feed on insects and spiders.

Flowers

The **high-casqued chameleon** dwells in the forests of eastern Africa. It gets its name from the tall helmet-like crest, or casque, on its head. This lizard is about six inches (15 centimeters) long, and it can extend its tongue farther than its body length. It uses this long, sticky tongue to snag insects and spiders.

A bee or butterfly approaches a flower for a sip of tasty nectar. Waiting there is a **white-banded crab spider.** When the unlucky insect gets close enough, the spider will be the one that gets a meal. This tricky spider is found throughout much of North America. The female spider's body is less than half an inch (1¼ centimeters) long. Male spiders are much smaller.

The **orchid mantis** lives in the rainforests of Southeast Asia. It looks almost exactly like part of an orchid flower. It ambushes insects as well as frogs, lizards, and other small animals. This fierce predator, which reaches 2½ inches (6 centimeters) in length, can hunt prey larger than itself.

The **wavy-lined emerald moth caterpillar** eats flowers and leaves. It camouflages itself with bits of whatever plant it is feeding on. The caterpillar is about ¾ inch (2 centimeters) long. It is found throughout much of the United States and southern Canada.

The **eyelash viper** gets its name from the scales that stick out above its eyes. This venomous snake often lurks among colorful flowers and fruit. When hunting, it will grab any bat, bird, or rodent that comes near. These snakes can be as much as 30 inches (76 centimeters) long. They live in the trees of Central and South American rainforests.

The **rainbow lorikeet** is about 12 inches (30 centimeters) long. It feeds on fruit, pollen, and nectar in the forests of eastern Australia, where its colorful plumage blends in with the flowers and foliage.

It also eats insects and their larvae.

Forest floor

The deadly **Gaboon viper** isn't easy to spot as it coils among the leaves and litter of the forest floor. This large, venomous snake is as much as six and a half feet (2 meters) long. Its fangs can be 2 inches (5 centimeters) long—the longest of any snake. It preys on birds and small mammals.

Adult **Malayan tapirs** have a striking black-and-white coat. But young tapirs are a dappled brown and white, a color scheme that helps them stay hidden on the forest floor. They live in Southeast Asia. When full-grown, these plant-eaters can be up to eight feet (2½ meters) long.

Its fringe of spines and dull, splotchy colors makes the **bat-faced toad** look like a

dead leaf. This amphibian is up to three inches (7½ centimeters) long. It spends its time on the forest floor in the jungles of South America, where it hunts for insects and spiders.

The wings of the **dead-leaf moth** are flat, but they look like a curled leaf—an amazing optical illusion. This insect has a wingspan of about two inches (5 centimeters). It lives in the forests and fields of central China, where its larvae feed on the leaves of walnut trees.

The **leaf-mimic katydid** is another insect that imitates a leaf. It also feeds on the leaves of trees and shrubs. This katydid is about one inch (2½ centimeters) long. It lives in the forests of Central and South America.

Arctic

The **willow grouse** lives in Alaska, northern Canada, northern Europe, and

Siberia. It is mostly brown in the summer, but it turns white with a few dark feathers during the winter. These birds are about 15 inches (38 centimeters) long. They feed on leaves, seeds, berries, and insects.

The **Arctic hare**, which makes its home in northern Canada and Greenland, stays active through the long winters. Its thick fur keeps it warm as it feeds on moss, twigs, roots, and other plant foods. Arctic hares average 22 inches (56 centimeters) in length, and can run at speeds of 40 miles per hour (64 kilometers per hour).

The **Arctic fox** also lives in the harsh conditions of northern Canada and Alaska. This carnivore hunts birds, fish, and hares throughout the year. If prey is scarce, it will eat carrion (dead animals) as well as berries and seaweed. These foxes are about two feet (61 centimeters) long.

Along with the Kodiak brown bear, the **polar bear** is the largest predator living on land. It can be nine feet (2³/₄ meters) long and weigh as much as 1,700 pounds (771 kilograms). It lives in the frigid lands that surround the Arctic Ocean. Polar bears are good swimmers. Seals are their favorite prey, but they will also attack and consume walruses and beluga whales. If there is no prey, they will eat bird eggs and plants.

Leaves and vines

The **elm sphinx moth** lives in the fields and forests of southern Canada and the eastern and Midwestern United States. Its larva, shown here, is about three inches (7¹/₂ centimeters) long. This caterpillar feeds on the leaves of elms and other trees. When it first emerges from its egg, the larva is bright green. After a few weeks, it turns a reddish-brown color.

It's easy to see how the **giant leaf insect** got its name. It lives in the forests of Southeast Asia, where it eats the leaves of trees. It can be more than four inches (10 centimeters) long. These insects are all females—they do not need a male to have offspring.

Found throughout Europe, the **green huntsman spider** preys on flies and other insects. It does not build a web, but uses its camouflage to remain hidden from its prey. Its body is about one-half inch (1¹/₄ centimeters) long. For a human, this spider's bite is painful but not serious.

The **green vine snake** coils among the branches of trees in the Central and South American rainforests. Its body is very thin, but can reach six and a half feet (2 meters) in length. It is a venomous snake, and it uses its disguise and its

venom to catch, kill, and eat frogs, lizards, and birds.

The **common brimstone butterfly** lives in the wetlands and wooded areas of Europe, Asia, and North Africa. It has a wingspan of two inches (5 centimeters) and it feeds on flower nectar.

At six and a half inches (16¹/₂ centimeters) in length, the **marsh frog** is large enough to prey on small birds, fish, and rodents. Insects and worms, however, are its main diet. This amphibian lives near fresh water in Europe and western Asia.

Though it looks frightening, the **satanic leaf gecko** is a shy insect-eater. It hunts at night in the forests of Madagascar. This lizard's amazing camouflage helps it hide from snakes, birds, and other predators. It can also shed its tail at will to confuse an attacker. It is about five inches (12¹/₂ centimeters) long.